DISCOVERING

GOD'S MYSTERIES

From the Bible-teaching ministry of

CHARLES R. SWINDOLL

INSIGHT FOR LIVING

Charles R. Swindoll graduated in 1963 from Dallas Theological Seminary, where he now serves as the school's fourth president, helping to prepare a new generation of men and women for the ministry. Chuck has served in pastorates in three states: Massachusetts, Texas, and California, including almost twenty-three years at the First Evangelical Free Church in Fullerton, California. He is currently senior pastor of Stonebriar Community Church in Frisco, Texas, north of Dallas. His sermon messages have been aired over radio since 1979 as the *Insight for Living* broadcast. A best-selling author, he has written numerous books and booklets on many subjects.

Based on the outlines and transcripts of Charles R. Swindoll's sermons, the study guide text was developed and written by the Educational Ministries Department at Insight for Living.

Editor in Chief:
Cynthia Swindoll

Study Guide Writer:
Jason Shepherd

Senior Editor and Assistant Writer:
Wendy Peterson

Editors:
Christina Grimstad
Karla Lenderink

Copy Editor:
Marco Salazar

Rights and Permissions:
The Meredith Agency

Text Designer:
Gary Lett

Graphic System Administrator:
Bob Haskins

Director, Communications Division:
John Norton

Print Production Manager:
Don Bernstein

Project Coordinator:
Jennifer Hubbard

Printer:
Sinclair Printing Company

Unless otherwise identified, all Scripture references are from the New American Standard Bible, updated edition, copyright © The Lockman Foundation 1960, 1962, 1963, 1968, 1971, 1972, 1973, 1975, 1977, 1995. Used by permission. Scripture taken from the Holy Bible, New International Version, Copyright © 1973, 1978, 1984 International Bible Society, used by permission of Zondervan Bible Publishers [NIV].

An effort has been made to locate sources and obtain permission where necessary for the quotations used in this book. In the event of any unintentional omission, a modification will gladly be incorporated in future printings.

ISBN 1-57972-347-0

Cover design: Strata Media

Cover image: © 2000 (Betsie Van de Meer)/Stone

Printed in the United States of America

CONTENTS

INTRODUCTION

What do you think of when you hear the word *mystery?* Does your mind wander to ponderables such as the impossible feats of a master magician like Harry Houdini? Or do you wonder about the seemingly unanswerable questions of why we're here and where all this is leading? There are a lot of things that remain unknown to us, a myriad of shadows that dance beyond the veil of our earth-bound intelligence.

But do you know that there is a different kind of mystery, a type of secret that can be understood, although it remains hidden to many? Would you like to know what it is? If you would, all you have to do is keep reading. This guide addresses that mystery and what you can do to understand much of it.

Take this journey with me. Together we'll peek behind the curtain of revelation—God's inerrant Word—and look full-faced into some of the secrets of God Himself. We'll peer into His character and find that while we cannot fully understand Him, we can know Him. I'll show you the mystery of the gospel and how it can be used powerfully in witnessing for Christ. You'll plumb the depths of the mystery of marriage—as God intended it—and surface with a whole new appreciation and commitment to love your spouse as God commands. And finally, we'll look into the future and discover another mystery: we'll learn the secrets of how Christians will be removed from this earth and how the antichrist will come and create lawlessness like this planet has never witnessed or endured.

So go ahead—turn the page. The answers to many mysteries await us!

Chuck Swindoll

Chuck Swindoll

PUTTING TRUTH
INTO ACTION

K nowledge apart from application falls short of God's desire for
His children. He wants us to apply what we learn so that we
will change and grow. This study guide was prepared with these
goals in mind. As you go through the following pages, we hope your
desire to discover biblical truth will grow as your understanding of
God's Word increases, and that you will be encouraged to apply
what you've learned.

   To assist you in your study, we've included a section called
S **Living Insights** at the end of each lesson. These exercises will
challenge you to study further and to think of specific ways to put
your discoveries into action.

   There are many ways to use this guide—in personal devotions,
group studies, discussions with friends and family, and Sunday school
classes. And, of course, it's an ideal study aid when you're listening
to its corresponding *Insight for Living* radio series.

   To benefit most from this study guide, we would encourage you
to consider it a spiritual journal. That's why we've included space
in the **Living Insights** for recording your thoughts and discoveries.
We hope you'll return to those sections often for review and en-
couragement as you continue to grow in your walk with Christ.

Insight for Living

DISCOVERING GOD'S MYSTERIES

Chapter 1

THE MYSTERY OF
GOD HIMSELF

Selected Scriptures

*M*ystery.

It's not the most comforting word, is it? A mystery, in fact, can be most unsettling. A searing pain in the throat that the doctors can't quite figure out . . . the unknown variables of a new job, a new town, a new home . . . or the deeper questions of who we are and why we're here.

We don't like these kinds of mysteries. Whether they are just a niggling question in the back of our minds or a change looming on the horizon, they threaten our stability, our happiness. They endanger the status quo that makes our lives so comfortable. They have a tendency to shake our foundations, to give rise to fear and anxiety.

Of course, some mysteries are easier to live with than others. We find it easier, for instance, to ponder, "Is there life in outer space?" than to wonder, "What's that lump in my breast?" Our distaste for a mystery is in direct proportion to its proximity to our lives. The farther away, the better.

Where, then, does that leave God? He's a mystery; that's for sure. His thoughts and ways are so far above our own that we cannot possibly understand them—He knows everything. In other words, He's *omniscient*. Likewise, His power is so far beyond our own that we can't even imagine the extent of it—He's *omnipotent*. Finally, He is present everywhere, *omnipresent*—a notion we cannot comprehend. Yes, God is a mystery, and like other mysteries, He has the potential to cause us great fear and anxiety. But we don't have to feel that way about Him.

Remember, God also loves us and wants the best for us. We can

1

rest in the fact that He knows the things that remain hidden to us. We can hide in the knowledge that He holds sway over the powers that lurk beyond our control, ruling sovereignly over the universe, even over the forces beyond our reach. We can be assured in His promise to walk beside us always, guiding and directing us, whatever comes our way.

God, the ultimate unknown, is our greatest comfort in the face of unknowns. So today, let's pull Him close and embrace Him. Let's look deeply into His eyes, drawing strength and comfort from the very things about Him that we cannot fully understand.

The Mystery of God

The mystery of God is such a big subject it's hard to decide where to begin. But perhaps the best place to start is with the book in the Bible that says more about God's mysteries than any other— the Book of Job.

God Is a Mystery . . .

You've read the story. A Satanic assault on Job's faith resulted in the loss of virtually everything he held dear: his property, his servants, even his children, and, finally his health. Covered with painful boils, bereft and grieving, Job was visited by three so-called "friends." Instead of comforting him, however, the three tried to convince Job that he had sinned against God in some way and was suffering as a result. Defending himself against this accusation, Job pointed to the mystery of God:

> "It is God who removes the mountains, they know
>   not how,
> When He overturns them in His anger;
> Who shakes the earth out of its place,
> And its pillars tremble;
> Who commands the sun not to shine,
> And sets a seal upon the stars;
> Who alone stretches out the heavens
> And tramples down the waves of the sea;
> Who makes the Bear, Orion and the Pleiades,
> And the chambers of the south;
> Who does great things, unfathomable,
> And wondrous works without number.
> (Job 9:5–10)

Job knew that he had lived righteously, and his three visitors could not convince him otherwise. Why, then, was he suffering? Job didn't know, but He could live with that. He didn't know how God made the earth or the heavens, and he didn't know why God allowed his suffering. In his own words, God was, to him, "unfathomable."

. . . Yet We Must Know Him

Job may not have known why God had allowed his suffering, but He knew God's character well enough that his faith in God—and his ability to take comfort in Him—did not waver. Though the Lord is a fathomless depth which we will never fully plumb, He is not inaccessible to us. We can become intimately acquainted with His personality, attributes, and desires by studying His Word, the Bible. Learning about God through the Bible is essential to our lives, and the omission of it can be our downfall, as J. I. Packer warns:

> Disregard the study of God, and you sentence yourself to stumble and blunder through life blindfolded.[1]

To ignore the study of God is to misread the universe in which we live. Pursuing knowledge of Him, on the other hand, breathes life and hope into our souls. As Charles Spurgeon was known to say:

> Confidence will be greatly sustained by a clear knowledge of God.[2]

Confidence—that's what Job had. How else could he stand against the accusations of his visitors while being devastated physically and emotionally as he was? And he didn't stumble and bumble through life blindfolded. Even when every physical reason for confidence was gone, stripped to nothing, he still hoped in God. And so can we, if we will learn all we can about the Creator of all good things—a Creator we can know and love.

The "Knowability" of God

If God is a mystery, what can we hope to understand about Him? Every reader of fiction knows that you learn about a character through what he says, what he does, and how others react to him. The Bible is not fiction—it is inspired, infallible truth—but it's also

---

1. J. I. Packer, *Knowing God* (Downers Grove, Ill.: InterVarsity Press, 1973), pp. 14-15.

2. Source unknown.

a story. Because it's a story, we can learn about God the way a reader learns about a character—by what God has said, what He has done, and how people have responded to Him. With this in mind, let's put on our reader's caps and observe two important truths about God.

His Rule Is Vast

Silent throughout most of the book of Job, toward the end, God finally speaks.

> Then the Lord answered Job out of the whirl-
> wind and said,
> "Who is this that darkens counsel
> By words without knowledge?
> Now gird up your loins like a man,
> And I will ask you, and you instruct Me!
> Where were you when I laid the foundation of the
>   earth?
> Tell Me, if you have understanding,
> Who set its measurements?
> Since you know.
> Or who stretched the line on it?
> On what were its bases sunk?
> Or who laid its cornerstone,
> When the morning stars sang together
> And all the sons of God shouted for joy?"
> (38:1–7)

The earth is enormous. Even with today's technology and centuries of scientific study, we know little about it. Yet God knows every inch of it. And the earth is but a speck in the vastness of what He knows.

> "Can you bind the chains of the Pleiades,
> Or loose the cords of Orion?
> Can you lead forth a constellation in its season,
> And guide the Bear with her satellites?
> Do you know the ordinances of the heavens,
> Or fix their rule over the earth?" (vv. 31–33)

To God, the distance between stars is nothing more than the width of His finger. To us, however, it is virtually unreachable. For example, if you were able to travel at the speed of light, you could arrive at the moon in 1 1/3 seconds. But continuing at that same speed,

4

do you know how long it would take you to reach the closest star? Four years! New York City's Hayden Planetarium offers us a tangible picture of the size of just our own solar system. The Planetarium

> has a miniature replica of our solar system show-
> ing the speeds and sizes of our planets. What is inter-
> esting is that the three outer planets are not even
> included. There wasn't room for Uranus, Neptune,
> and Pluto. Uranus would be in the planetarium's
> outer corridor, Neptune would be around Eighth Ave-
> nue. And Pluto? Another three long avenues away
> at Fifth Avenue. By the way, no stars are included,
> for obvious reasons. Can you imagine (on the same
> scale) where the nearest star would be located?
> Cleveland, Ohio. Vast! And, remember, that's just
> our own local galaxy.[3]

God's domain is indeed vast. But His care over that domain is meticulous.

His Care Is Meticulous

God knows all the stars by name, but He also knows the number of hairs on our heads (Matt. 10:30). Can you imagine that? Jason has 5,432 hairs. Jenny has 6,456, and poor Jackson—he has only 291. Although some of us may not be completely happy with the color, texture, or quantity of our hair, it's still amazing to know that the same God who swirls galaxies in His palm also knows each of us so intimately.

His care also extends to the microscopic world. For example, an electron, if it were increased in size until it became as large as an apple, and a human being grew larger in the same proportion, that person could hold the entire solar system in the palm of his hand and would have to use a magnifying glass in order to see it.[4]

God's care is meticulous—He's the maker of electrons and the counter of head hairs. Yet He's also vast—the engineer of galaxies. His knowledge is infinitely large, yet infinitely small. In other words, He's a paradox, an

> infinite circle whose center is everywhere and whose

3. Charles R. Swindoll, The Finishing Touch (Dallas, Tex.: Word Publishing, 1994), p. 276.

4. Haddon W. Robinson, Biblical Preaching (Grand Rapids, Mich.: Baker Book House, 1980), p. 143.

circumference is nowhere . . . . You are a God of
infinite power, and yet utterly merciful. You can hide
Yourself from us, and yet be with us all the time.
You are the creator of both raw energy and gentle
beauty. You never change, and yet You are the author of change everywhere. You are neither old nor
young, being eternal, yet You make all things new.
You are endlessly active, and yet the source of true
rest. You love totally, but without obsession. You
possess us completely, but without anxiety or domi-
nation. You owe us nothing, but You pay off all the
debt of our sins.[5]

How can we fully understand a God like that? How can we get
our arms around Him? We can't, but we can know Him to a degree,
and that should be the goal of our lives—to know and appreciate
Him as well as we can. Unfortunately, the times in which we live
make it especially hard for us to achieve that goal.

The Loss and Recapture of God

So much in our society today challenges our inclination to ex-
plore God's mysteries. We live in the information age—a time in
which humankind, through the wonder of science, seems to have
just about everything figured out. We understand what causes cancer; we can predict natural disasters; we're able to travel through
space. It seems that new discoveries take place every day. And all
that knowledge is at our fingertips; a click of our mouse links us to
experts on nearly anything. What need do we have of God? Yet inside
us, some little part of our heart yearns for something more than
information. We crave a connection to the Creator of this world we
are discovering so much about. We hope for a cure for cancer; but
we still need comfort when cancer strikes; we can watch a hurri-
cane's approach, but we still need arms to huddle in while it rages.

So how can we find that connection? Where can we feel those
arms? Three daily disciplines can put us in touch.

- First, *talk to God intimately every morning*. Start each day the
right way. Connect with God early, and you'll walk confidently

5. Attributed to St. Augustine, source unknown.

through the next twenty-four hours, knowing that the God you serve is bigger than the mysteries that await you.

- Second, *turn to Him throughout the day*. Every day is filled with unforeseen pressures, stresses, and troubles. Our natural tendency is to handle them ourselves, to solve them with our own knowledge, or endure them with our own strength. But why not lean on the One who is so much wiser and stronger than we are?

- Third, *reflect on your day and thank Him every night*. There's an old song that advises, "When you're worried and you can't sleep, just count your blessings instead of sheep." When bedtime comes, resist the temptation to fret about what's past or what is to come. Instead, reflect on all the ways God has cared for you during the day, and peace will take over. Not only that, but your connection to the Comforter will grow that much stronger as you dwell on the things He has done.

We can't escape the mysteries of life. As long as we walk this earth, we'll encounter undiagnosed illnesses, seemingly senseless tragedies, and other hardships that are beyond our finite comprehension. But nothing is beyond God's understanding. He is bigger than all the mysteries of the universe. And He loves us. And that's all we really need to know.

Living Insights

One of the best ways to know God better is to study His *attributes*. An attribute is an essential, permanent, and distinguishing quality of a person, and it's always confirmed by the person's words and actions. Take a few minutes to put on your reader's cap again and ponder some of God's attributes and how they've been revealed by His words and actions in the Bible.

Holiness (Exod. 19:1–17) _____

_____

_____

_____

Faithfulness (Rev. 21:1–6) _____

_____

7

Goodness (Matt. 7:7–11) _____

_____

_____

Mercy (Eph. 2:1–10) _____

_____

_____

Lovingkindness (John 3:16) _____

_____

_____

   In your reflection time, ponder how God has revealed one or
more of His attributes in His dealings with you today.

Chapter 2

THE MYSTERY OF
THE GOSPEL

Ephesians 2:1–16; 3:1–10; 6:1–20

In the early 1960s, people were shocked by the controversial book *Black Like Me*. It was written by John Howard Griffin—a white man who became black. After shaving his hair and temporarily changing his skin color through a series of medical treatments, the author walked, hitchhiked, and rode buses through the Deep South. His goal was to gather scientific data; but in the end, he filed that information away and published instead the journal he kept of his experiences.

In this journal he traced "the changes that occur to heart and body and intelligence when a so-called first-class citizen is cast on the junkheap of second-class citizenship."[1] He had found that many people who normally would have treated him with courtesy and gracious hospitality subjected him instead to insults, mistreatment, and a hate so raw it could only be described as violent. For Griffin had walked, hitchhiked, and ridden buses down a main thoroughfare of human depravity—prejudice. Listen to the preface of his book.

> The Negro. The South. These are details. The real story is the universal one of men who destroy the souls and bodies of other men (and in the process destroy themselves) for reasons neither really understands. It is the story of the persecuted, the defrauded, the feared and detested. I could have been a Jew in Germany, a Mexican in a number of states, or a member of any "inferior" group. Only the details would have differed. The story would be the same.[2]

To be completely fair about this volatile subject, we should note that we can always find prejudice on both sides. Yes, there are whites against blacks, but there are also blacks against whites. There

---

1. John Howard Griffin, *Black Like Me*, 2nd ed. (Boston, Mass.: Houghton Mifflin Co., 1977), preface.

2. Griffin, *Black Like Me*, preface.

are rich against poor and poor against rich. Men against women and vice versa. Jews and Gentiles, and Protestants and Catholics. On and on we could go, for prejudice exists wherever lines of distinction are drawn—between races, cultures, religions, and classes.[3]

We don't like to admit it, but we all have our little prejudices. If we don't subscribe to any of the biggies mentioned above, then we likely harbor more subtle prejudices, such as intolerance toward people of certain personality types or political views. What about people who belong to different denominations or who wear different kinds of clothes?

It's not strange or unusual for us to fear or even loathe others who are different than ourselves. But the Bible lays out a very different plan for God's people. In God's family, there is no rich or poor, no Jew or Greek, no freedman or slave. We're all one—all on the same level. The Bible calls this the "mystery" of the gospel. It's an important part of God's Good News, so let's take some time to examine first the gospel and then the mystery it contains.

The Dark Backdrop of the Gospel

Any discussion of the gospel must begin with a description of sin, and that's exactly what Paul offers in his letter to the Ephesians.

Dead in Trespasses and Sins

Just as a painter begins his work on the canvas by creating a background, Paul begins his presentation of the gospel by describing the dark spiritual condition of all people.

> And you were dead in your trespasses and sins.
> (Eph. 2:1)

Does it puzzle you that Paul describes as "dead" people who look very much alive? After all, many professional athletes have never heard of Christ, yet they stand as living monuments to physical vitality and health. And what about the many geniuses living today? Many of them have never prayed, read the Bible, or gone to church, yet they are much more alert and productive than the average person. How can Paul claim these people are dead?

3. The preceding part of this chapter has been adapted from "Christ at the Crossroads of Prejudice" in the study guide *Christ at the Crossroads*, coauthored by Lee Hough, from the Bible-teaching ministry of Charles R. Swindoll (Anaheim, Calif.: Insight for Living, 1998).

He can do so because these people, if they have never believed in Christ, are dead in the most important way—they're dead spiritually. They are

> blind to the glory of Jesus Christ, and deaf to the voice of the Holy Spirit. They have no love for God, no sensitive awareness of his personal reality, no leaping of their spirit towards him in the cry, 'Abba, Father', no longing for fellowship with his people. They are as unresponsive to him as a corpse. So we should not hesitate to affirm that a life without God (however physically fit and mentally alert a person may be) is a living death, and that those who live it are dead even while they are living.[4]

How, specifically, are these people spiritually dead? They're dead in their "trespasses and sins." These two terms, carefully chosen by Paul, give a thorough account of the unsaved condition. A "trespass," *paraptōma* in Greek, denotes a false step—one taken either by crossing an unknown boundary or by deviating from a known path. A "sin" (*hamartia*), however, refers to missing the mark, falling short of a standard.[5] Together, the two words cover both the active and passive aspects of spiritual death. In God's eyes, the unsaved are rebels and failures, and as a result, are "dead"—alienated from Him.

Living as Unbelievers

Paul adds detail to the backdrop by describing humanity's fallen condition. He specifically relates it to the past of his Ephesian readers.

> In which you formerly walked according to the course of this world, according to the prince of the power of the air, of the spirit that is now working in the sons of disobedience. Among them we too all formerly lived in the lusts of our flesh, indulging the desires of the flesh and of the mind, and were by nature children of wrath, even as the rest. (vv. 2–3)

---

4. John R. W. Stott, *The Message of Ephesians*, The Bible Speaks Today series (Downers Grove, Ill.: InterVarsity Press, 1979), p. 72.

5. Stott, *The Message of Ephesians*, p. 71.

Before the Ephesian believers came to Christ, they were spiritually dead, and Paul notes that their lives were characterized by three distinctive marks[6]:

- *They walked according to the course of this world.* "Walked" refers to the general direction of a person's life, and "course of this world" indicates a whole value system or worldview that is alien to God.[7] The Ephesians, prior to salvation, lived in and contributed to a society devoid of godly direction.

- *They followed the prince of the power of the air.* This prince is Satan. The Greek term for prince, *archon*, highlights Satan's control, which he exercises over "the air," *tou aeros*—the space over the earth. In other words, Satan's sphere of influence extends over the entire face of the world—which includes the lives of all people. Without Christ's power, unbelievers are susceptible to Satan's control. The Ephesians, like all unsaved people, followed him whether they knew it or not, and they usually didn't.

- *They gratified the lusts of their flesh.* These "lusts" are the natural cravings of the sinful nature. They include ragings, sexual promiscuity, materialism, and the like.

As a result of their unredeemed condition, Paul says the Ephesians were "children of wrath." They were at enmity with God. They were destined for judgment and hell. And so are all of us who have not trusted in Christ for the forgiveness of our sins. This is a harrowing truth. It's the dark backdrop of the gospel. Fortunately, Paul does not leave us without hope.

The Bright, Mysterious Light of the Gospel

Upon the dark canvas he has painted, Paul begins adding strokes of pure light.

The Gospel

With two words, the apostle changes everything. Verse four

---

6. Bruce B. Barton, Philip Comfort, Kent Keller, Linda K. Taylor, and Dave Veerman, *Ephesians*, Life Application Bible Commentary series (Wheaton, Ill.: Tyndale House Publishers, Inc., 1996), pp. 38–39.

7. Stott, *The Message of Ephesians*, p. 73.

begins, "But God." The whole sentence reads:

> But God, being rich in mercy, because of His great love with which He loves us, even when we were dead in our transgressions, made us alive together with Christ (by grace you have been saved), and raised us up with Him, and seated us with Him in the heavenly places in Christ Jesus, so that in the ages to come He might show the surpassing riches of His grace in kindness toward us in Christ Jesus. (vv. 4–7)

The first two words are perhaps the most welcome in all of Scripture. These two syllables, set against the desperate condition of fallen humankind, introduce the glorious light of the gospel. We were dead in our sins, *but God* . . . . We were rebels against Him, *but God* . . . . We were enslaved by Satan and our own sinful flesh, *but God* . . . . What a wonderful turnaround! And it gets even better.

The remainder of these verses contain three main verbs, which describe actions God has taken on our behalf:

- He has made us alive (v. 5).

- He has raised us up (v. 6a).

- He has seated us in the heavenly places (v. 6b).

Each of these proclamations is accompanied by the prepositional phrase "with Christ." By virtue of our new union with Christ, we actually share in His resurrection, ascension, and rule in heaven. These three benefits are the *products* of the gospel, but what is the gospel itself? Paul explains:

> For by grace you have been saved through faith; and that not of yourselves, it is the gift of God; not as a result of works, so that no one may boast. For we are His workmanship, created in Christ Jesus for good works, which God prepared beforehand so that we would walk in them. (vv. 8–10)

Simply put, the gospel consists of three facts: 1) We are all sinners and deserve to be eternally separated from God; 2) God sent His Son Jesus to die as payment for our sin; and 3) Each one of us must believe in Him and His payment in order to receive eternal life. As Paul emphasized, there is no good work we can perform to earn our salvation. Rather, the good works we were

13

created to do for His glory come as a *result* of our salvation, not as a *prerequisite* of it.

The Mystery of the Gospel

In addition to this gospel message, Paul reminds the Ephesians of the ethnic division that existed between themselves and the Jews, a division that Christ came to tear down.

> Therefore remember that formerly you, the Gentiles in the flesh, who are called "Uncircumcision" by the so-called "Circumcision," which is performed in the flesh by human hands—remember that you were at that time separate from Christ, excluded from the commonwealth of Israel, and strangers to the covenants of promise, having no hope and without God in the world. But now in Christ Jesus you who formerly were far off have been brought near by the blood of Christ. For He Himself is our Peace, who made both groups into one and broke down the barrier of the dividing wall, by abolishing in His flesh the enmity, which is the Law of commandments contained in ordinances, so that in Himself he might make the two into one new man, thus establishing peace, and might reconcile them both in one body to God through the cross, by it having put to death the enmity. (vv. 11–16)

When Paul referred to the "dividing wall," he was not speaking metaphorically. There was a real wall commonly referred to by that name.

> It was a notable feature of the magnificent temple built in Jerusalem by Herod the Great. The temple building itself was constructed on an elevated platform. Round it was the Court of the Priests. East of this was the Court of Israel, and further east the court of the women. These three courts—for the priests, the lay men and the lay women of Israel respectively—were all on the same elevation as the temple itself. From this level one descended five steps to a walled platform, and then on the other side of the wall fourteen more steps to another wall,

beyond which was the outer court or Court of the Gentiles . . . From any part of it the Gentiles could look up and view the temple, but were not allowed to approach it. They were cut off from it by the surrounding wall, which was a one-and-a-half metre stone barricade, on which were displayed at intervals warning notices in Greek and Latin. They read, in effect, not "Trespassers will be prosecuted" but "Trespassers will be executed."[8]

The divisiveness that existed in Paul's day was just as bad as, if not worse than, the racism we have seen in our own times. Whether old or new, Christ's intention is to destroy it. Paul continues:

For this reason I, Paul, the prisoner of Christ Jesus for the sake of you Gentiles—if indeed you have heard of the stewardship of God's grace which was given to me for you; that by revelation there was made known to me the mystery, as I wrote before in brief. By referring to this, when you read you can understand my insight into the mystery of Christ, which in other generations was not made know to the sons of men, as it has now been revealed to His holy apostles and prophets in the Spirit; to be specific, that the Gentiles are fellow heirs and fellow members of the body, and fellow partakers of the promise in Christ Jesus through the gospel, of which I was made a minister, according to the gift of God's grace which was given to me according to the working of His power. To me, the very least of all saints, this grace was given, to preach to the Gentiles the unfathomable riches of Christ, and to bring to light what is the administration of the mystery which for ages has been hidden in God who created all things; so that the manifold wisdom of God might now be made known through the church to the rulers and the authorities in the heavenly places. (3:1–10)

Several times, Paul uses the term *mystery, mystērion* in the Greek. The word may deceive us if we don't pay close attention.

8. Stott, *The Message of Ephesians*, pp. 91–92.

15

In English, a mystery is something dark, obscure, secret, or puzzling. What is mysterious is inexplicable, even incomprehensible. The Greek term, however, referred to something that was secret but could be understood and embraced with the proper initiation.[9] The mystery, as Paul defined it, is the complete union of Jews and Gentiles with each other through the union of both with Christ. This double union, with Christ and with each other, is the substance of the mystery.[10]

This mystery still applies to us today. As God's people, we make up a single body, even though we are often very different from each other. We possess different skin tones, speak different languages, and often participate in a wide variety of ordinances, but we're unified by our Head. This is something that our world cannot understand. It's a mystery to them.

Even with the recent emphasis on tolerance and multicultural-ism, modern society has found it impossible to stamp out prejudice and racism. Unity is still a mystery to this world, and it will continue to be so. Only by being initiated into the mystery of the gospel, which comes through faith in Christ, can anyone obtain the knowl-edge and power needed to overcome division. Not until Christ returns to rule will division be permanently quelled. Until then, the universal story of *Black Like Me* will continue to take place in the "Deep Souths" of this world. But we, as one body in Christ, can continue to shine God's light in the dark places because we understand the mystery of the gospel and have the power to over-come all the walls that divide.

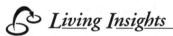 Living Insights

Even Christians struggle with prejudice. John Stott once wrote, "Our old nature is no more extinct than the devil, but God's will is that the dominion of both should be broken."[11] The old nature will continue to entice us to follow its lead. One of the best ways to combat it is by recognizing that we're in a war with our flesh.

---

9. Stott, *The Message of Ephesians*, p. 116.

10. Stott, *The Message of Ephesians*, p. 117.

11. John R. W. Stott as quoted by Barton, Comfort, Keller, Taylor, and Veerman in *Ephesians*, p. 39.

Take a moment to read Ephesians 6:10–20, considering how the armor of God can help you fight the prejudices you lean toward:

Belt of Truth
How can you equip yourself with God's truth so that you can identify counterfeit versions of tolerance and unity?

_____

_____

_____

Breastplate of Righteousness
How can you guard your heart from unrighteous, divisive feelings?

_____

_____

_____

Shoes of Peace
How can you share the gospel by walking in peace?

_____

_____

_____

Shield of Faith
How can you protect yourself from Satan's assaults on your unity with other believers?

_____

_____

_____

Helmet of Salvation
How can you protect your mind from adopting prejudices or racist thinking?

_____

_____

Sword of God's Word
How can reading, studying, and memorizing the Word help you understand the mystery of the gospel?

_____

_____

_____

Now that you know what the mystery of the gospel is and how to attain it, pray as Paul did—that God will give you the courage and strength to root out any hint of prejudice in your own life and in your local community of believers.

Chapter 3

THE MYSTERY OF MARRIAGE
PART ONE
Genesis 2:21–25; Ephesians 5:22–33

You probably weren't all that surprised to read in Chapter One that the Bible describes God as a mystery. And maybe you weren't too shocked to find in Chapter Two that God's gospel message contains one. But did you realize that Scripture teaches that marriage is a mystery too? It does. In fact, Paul identifies the husband-wife bond as just that in the same letter in which he proclaimed the mystery of the gospel.

In Ephesians 5 the apostle, referring to marriage, writes "This *musterion* is great" (v. 32). By "great," he didn't mean that the secret of marital union is wonderful, although it certainly is. Rather, he meant there is something about it that is deep, profound. The Latin version of the Bible, Jerome's Vulgate, uses the term *magnum* for "great," which today we might render "mega."

How is marriage a "mega-mystery"? Simply stated, the bond between a man and a woman is a model of the relationship between God and His people. God instituted marriage to act as a microcosm of the larger relationship between Himself and humanity. As such, the interactions between husband and wife should exemplify the same love, acceptance, grace, and joy that God exhibits in His dealings with us. This is the mystery of marriage, and God wants us to reveal His love to the world through the way we love our spouses.

How, specifically, can we make our marriages models of godly love? The Lord Himself tells us in two passages of Scripture—one in the Old Testament, one in the New.

Four Principles of a "Mysterious" Marriage

If we're going to study marriage, we might as well start with the first one—Adam and Eve's. Genesis 2 marks the inception of their union and contains four principles for a godly marriage.

Before we look at these four principles, however, we need to remind ourselves of one important fact: *there's a big difference between a principle and a rule*. A rule lays down black-and-white boundaries —"Speed Limit: 35 MPH." A principle, on the other hand, points us in a general direction—"Danger, Curve Ahead." See the difference? A rule tells you exactly what you can and can't do and usually implies some kind of punishment for failure to comply. A principle, though, gives you basic advice and does so with the promise of helping you achieve the best.

Most of God's instructions concerning marriage consist of principles, not rules. He doesn't tell us, "Thou shalt love your mate, lest your life be short and miserable." No, He gives us principles that will help our marriages bloom with all the love and grace and joy He designed them to. With this important distinction in mind, let's look at the four principles He offers.

Severance

First, God tells us that marriage partners must sever themselves from their parents before they can join to each other. After describing the creation of Eve for Adam (vv. 21–23), the Scripture says,

> For this reason a man shall *leave* his father and his mother . . . (v. 24a, emphasis added)

This sounds simple, and yet it's so hard for some people to do. The Hebrew term for "leave," *āzab*, means "to depart." In other contexts, it means "forsake." Proverbs 28:13 talks about "forsaking" sin, for instance; and Deuteronomy 28:20 refers to people "forsaking" God.[1] "Leaving" means more than merely changing an address. It means removing yourself from your parents' authority or control.

Does this mean that married people should "forsake" their parents in all ways, never speaking to them again? Obviously not. The parent-child relationship can continue to grow in many ways, but it must change in others. Especially, it must evolve from an authority relationship to a mentoring one.

How many times have men failed to "leave" their parents by constantly comparing their wives to their mothers or by continually caving in to their fathers' demands? And how many times have women failed to "leave" their parents by constantly saying to their husbands, "Daddy never did it that way" or "Mom says we should

---

1. R. Laird Harris, Gleason L. Archer, Jr., and Bruce K. Waltke, eds., *Theological Wordbook of the Old Testament* (Chicago, Ill.: Moody Press, 1980), vol. 2, pp. 658–659.

do it this way." These mates have not severed from their mothers and fathers.

If we refuse to make that separation, our marriages will never bloom the way God designed them to—they'll never have the chance. Rather, they'll be smothered by of unfair and unrealistic expectations. Instead of appreciating our spouses for all the wonderful things they are and do, we'll continually be disappointed with them. They'll never measure up or match the unspoken expectations we have for them. How unfortunate! God meant our marriages to be so much more. And He set the example for us by refraining from comparing us to other believers.

Permanence

Next we find the second principle for a "mysterious" marriage:

. . . and [a man shall] *be joined* to his wife (Gen. 2:24b, emphasis added)

The term "be joined," or "cleave" is a strong word in Hebrew. It conveys the idea of permanence.

> *dābaq* ["be joined"] is used quite often in the OT of physical things sticking to each other, especially parts of the body. Job says that his bone cleaves to his skin (19:20). . . .
>
> In God's description of leviathan, he mentions that "the flakes of his flesh are joined together" (Job 41:23), referring to the plates of a crocodile's skin or the scales of a snake. . . .
>
> *dābaq* also carries the sense of clinging to someone in affection and loyalty. Man is to cleave to his wife (Gen 2:24). Ruth clave to Naomi (Ruth 1:14). The men of Judah clave to David their king during Sheba's rebellion (II Sam 20:2). . . .
>
> Most importantly, the Israelites are to cleave to the Lord in affection and loyalty (Deut 10:20; 11:22; 13:4; 30:20; Josh 22:5; 23:8) if his blessing is to be theirs.[2]

Just as a bone and flesh are permanently attached—and just as

---

2. R. Laird Harris, Gleason L. Archer, Jr., and Bruce K. Waltke, eds., *Theological Wordbook of the Old Testament*, (Chicago, Ill.: Moody Press, 1980), vol. 1, pp. 177–178.

God is permanently in our lives—so are marriage partners to be forever united. Unfortunately, some couples achieve permanence not through godly love but out of a sense of duty. Staying together without actively loving each other no more fulfills God's design for marriage than does splitting up. Willard F. Harley Jr., in his classic book on marriage, *His Needs, Her Needs: Building an Affair-Proof Marriage* notes that lasting and loving marriages don't result from the amount of passion two people feel for each other in the beginning. Rather, permanent relationships are formed when two people take meticulous care of each others' needs over the long haul. Permanence in marriage results from learning what those needs are, learning how to meet them, and making the effort to do so.

How many couples do you know who consistently do those things? The ones who do irresistibly represent part of the mystery of God's relationship with us.

Unity

Next, we're told that unity is an essential ingredient.

> . . . and they shall become *one flesh.* (v. 24c, emphasis added)

What does it mean to become "one flesh"? Based on the teaching of the Old Testament, we can surmise that it means a likemindedness, a oneness of emotions, will, and spirit.[3] Today, we might describe it as operating on the same frequency or being on the same page. When we're unified with our spouses, we have a singular purpose—to glorify and serve God through our marriages. And as a result, we act in harmony with each other.

Easier said than done. After all, men and women are *very* different. Men tend to be bigger and firmer while women tend to be smaller and softer; men produce testosterone and women estrogen. And those are just the physical differences! Men and women tend to approach virtually every aspect of life in different ways. Moreover, each couple has to work through a plethora of individual idiosyncrasies: family history, cultural backgrounds, denominational affiliation, personality type, and so on. With all of these dissimilarities working against us, how are we supposed to become "one flesh"

---

3. Edward G. Dobson, *What the Bible Really Says about Marriage, Divorce and Remarriage* (Old Tappan, New Jersey: Fleming H. Revell Company, 1986), p. 22.

with our spouses? We become unified with them in the same way that we become like-minded with all believers:

> To sum up, all of you be harmonious, sympathetic, brotherly, kindhearted, and humble in spirit; not returning evil for evil or insult for insult, but giving a blessing instead. (1 Pet. 3:8)

Want harmony with your spouse? Treat him or her with sympathy, loyalty, kindness, humility, grace, and forgiveness. You may never be alike, but you'll find it easier to become "one flesh."

Intimacy

The fourth principle is intimacy.

> And the man and his wife were both naked and were not ashamed. (Gen. 2:25)

In their sinless condition, Adam and Eve had no barriers between them—in other words, no clothes. They had no need of them since they could be completely free and open with each other without fear of being hurt or abused.

At the Fall, however, sex became distorted, with the potential to be used in ungodly ways. Clothing then acted as a restrainer of humanity's newfound sin nature and its lustful desires. But it also represented the presence of sin, an obstacle to intimacy—a barrier that every believer from then on would have to overcome to achieve intimacy in his or her marriage.

Although we live in a fallen world and struggle against lust as much as ever, God still wants us to reflect the naked intimacy He created between Adam and Eve. To achieve that level of intimacy, however, we need to feel safe in our marriages. We need to feel cherished and protected, without fear of being judged, rejected, abused, or taken for granted. For this to happen, we need to know more about how to nurture intimacy. Ephesians offers us some help in that area.

Wise Words to Marriage Partners

In Ephesians, Paul paints a beautiful picture of marriage as God intended it. By giving just two simple instructions—one to wives and one to husbands—he gives us the knowledge we need to have greater intimacy as well as more unity and permanence.

To Wives

> Wives, be subject to your own husbands, as to
> the Lord. For the husband is the head of the wife,
> as Christ also is the head of the church, He Himself
> being the Savior of the body. But as the church is
> subject to Christ, so also the wives ought to be to
> their husbands in everything. (5:22–24)

The single command God gives to women is to *submit to their husbands*. Perhaps no command in Scripture has been as misused as this one. Over the ages, selfish and power-hungry men have used it to manipulate and dominate well-intentioned women. What a tragedy!

Before we look more closely at this command, let's be sure we understand two things. First, it should be taken in conjunction with the command to husbands, and vice-versa. Just as a bird must have two wings to fly, for marriage to soar as God intended, both men and women must do their parts. A selfish man will ground a marriage no matter how submissive his wife is, and a defiant woman will cause a marriage to flounder no matter how loving and sacrificial her husband is.

Second, the failings of one spouse usually does not give the other an excuse to stop trying. Extreme cases aside (infidelity, physical and/or emotional abuse, and so on), God wants us to keep loving and submitting although our spouse may not be reciprocating. Look at Peter's words on this issue:

> You wives, be submissive to your own husbands so
> that even if any of them are disobedient to the word,
> they may be won without a word by the behavior
> of their wives, as they observe your chaste and re-
> spectful behavior. . . .
> You husbands in the same way, live with your
> wives in an understanding way. (1 Pet. 3:1–2; 7a)

According to Peter, when one partner slacks off, the other should not slack off also but redouble his or her efforts to "win" the wayward spouse back.

In light of these two truths, let's now look at the command to women. What does it mean to "be subject" to a husband? Submission is no stranger to the Christian. Every believer is expected to submit to God (James 4:7), to church leaders (Heb. 13:17), and to each other (Eph. 5:21). To submit, in general, means to place yourself under the authority of someone who occupies a position worthy of respect, such as a parent, boss, or civil leader.[4] Specifically applied to a married woman, it means "willingly following her husband's leadership in Christ."[5]

With this in mind, women, consider the following reasons to submit to your husbands in a godly manner:

- First, *submission in marriage is a function of creation, not culture.* Many women disregard the Bible's commands for them to submit because they claim those commands applied only to the ancient cultures in which the Bible was written. However, Scripture makes it clear that God commands women to submit because that is the order He established at creation.[6]

- Second, *marital submission is a reflection of all believers' subjection to Christ.* Submission is one way in which the mystery of marriage is lived out. When wives submit to their husbands, they reflect the way all Christians subject themselves to Christ.

- Third, *submission is commanded by Scripture.* There are times when submission seems archaic and even illogical. After all, men are not unanimously smarter than women or better at making decisions. But the purpose of submission is larger than just the current issue at hand. It's a principle that makes marriages run more smoothly and that exhibits the way God's relationship is supposed to work with His church, or Bride. It would take more space than is available here to discuss the reasons submission is a good thing, but the most compelling one can be stated simply: God calls for it in His Word.

To the Husbands

Now let's look at God's command to the men.

Husbands, love your wives, just as Christ also loved the church and gave Himself up for her . . .

---

4. Walter Bauer, *A Greek-English Lexicon of the New Testament and Other Early Christian Literature*, trans. William F. Arndt and F. Wilbur Gingrich (Chicago, Ill.: University of Chicago Press, 1979), p. 848.

5. Bruce B. Barton, Philip Comfort, Kent Keller, Linda K. Taylor and Dave Veerman, *Ephesians*, Life Application Bible Commentary series (Wheaton, Ill.: Tyndale House Publishers, 1996), p. 113.

6. For further study, read 1 Cor. 11:1–22. In this passage, a head covering is a physical expression of a woman's submission to her husband.

> So husbands ought also to love their own wives as
> their own bodies. He who loves his own wife loves
> himself; for no one ever hated his own flesh, but
> nourishes and cherishes it, just as Christ also does
> the church, because we are members of His body.
> (Eph. 5:25, 28–30)

The single command God gives to men is for them to *love their
wives*. To help the men understand the requirements of this command, God gives two analogies. First, he tells men to love their
wives as Christ loved the church (v. 25). That's quite a standard,
isn't it? Simply stated, men ought to be willing to die for their
wives; more importantly, though, they ought to *live* for them. Men
ought to draw every breath, not to fulfill their own needs or desires,
but for the purpose of serving and cherishing their women.

To make this point more graphically, God brings it a little closer
to home. He tells husbands to love their wives as they love their
own bodies (v. 28). What normal man doesn't feed his body, rest
his body, and make sure that it's as comfortable as possible at all
times? God commands husbands to seek their wives' comfort before
their own, to continually keep an eye out for her needs and desires,
to cherish and nourish her—always and forever. Sometimes it
means doing more chores around the house. Sometimes it means
taking care of the kids so she can meet some friends for coffee. It
always means a life of loving servitude that models the service
Christ performed for the sake of the church.

In this way, husbands can live out the mystery of marriage. Just
as Christ loved the church, they can love their wives. And the wives
can live out the mystery as well by submitting to their husbands'
loving leadership. These are just two ways in which spouses can
reveal to the world the way in which God relates to all mankind.

𝒞ℴ *Living Insights*

Take a minute to evaluate your marriage in the four areas discussed in Genesis. On a scale of 1 to 10, where does your marriage
stand? How can you improve?

Severance

1	2	3	4	5	6	7	8	9	10
(non-existent)									(perfect)

In what areas do you need to sever ties with your parents?

_____

_____

_____

_____

_____

Permanence

1	2	3	4	5	6	7	8	9	10
(non-existent)									(perfect)

In what ways can you take meticulous care of your spouse's needs in order to cleave more closely to him or her?

_____

_____

_____

_____

_____

Unity

1	2	3	4	5	6	7	8	9	10
(non-existent)									(perfect)

What differences between you and your spouse seem to give you the most trouble? How can you overcome these differences?

_____

_____

_____

_____

_____

Intimacy

1	2	3	4	5	6	7	8	9	10
(non-existent)									(perfect)

If you're a woman, in what ways can you show greater submission to your husband? If you're a man, how can you love your wife in a more Christlike way?

_____

_____

_____

_____

Chapter 4

THE MYSTERY OF MARRIAGE
PART TWO
Genesis 2, 3; 1 Corinthians 7:1–5

In the last chapter, we learned about one of the mysteries of marriage —that it reflects the larger relationship between God and His children. But there is another mystery as well. As Jay Kesler writes:

> When a man and woman become one in marriage, their marriage becomes a symbol of the unity of the Godhead. Their relationship enables them to understand more of the nature of God's personality than either one would be able to understand alone. . . . When two become one in marriage, the door is opened that allows them to refine human relationships to the degree that they can begin to understand more of God's nature. . . .
>
> I believe the marriage relationship is intended, at its most foundational level, to open to human beings the opportunity of knowing God at a glorified, deeper level—and also to grow in knowledge of one another.[1]

What does all that mean? A committed marriage reflects the character of God. It gives married people an opportunity to understand God in a deeper way—and it can also help them improve their marriages as they imitate Him. Let's turn again to the story of creation and learn even more about God's wonderful design for marriage.

God's Pattern for Marriage

The world God created was perfect, including the marriage between Adam and Eve. Their relationship exhibited the way God intended for a man and woman to bond together perfectly—at least, at first.

1. Jay Kesler, "Marriage Teaches about God" in *Husband and Wives*, ed. Howard and Jeanne Hendricks, with LaVonne Neff (Wheaton, Ill.: Victor Books, 1988), p.29.

God's Perfect Plan

Genesis 2 has already shown us some important facets of a godly marriage: severance, permanence, unity, and intimacy. But it offers us still one more. Today, we see that a good marriage relationship is based on commitment and loyalty, not merely feelings. Look at what Adam says after seeing Eve and realizing she is God's gift to him.

"This is now bone of my bones,
And flesh of my flesh;
She shall be called Woman,
Because she was taken out of Man." (Gen. 2:23)

These are the first words spoken by a human that are recorded in the Bible. Doesn't it seem significant that they were in regard to marriage? Surely that tells us of the importance of marriage in God's eyes. And the words themselves reveal one of the pillars of a godly marriage—commitment.

The image Adam used, shared bone and flesh, is a covenant formula, and it speaks not just of a common heritage but of a reciprocal loyalty. We see it used again in 2 Samuel 5:1, where representatives of the northern tribe of Israel visit David at Hebron and say to him, "we are your bone and flesh." These men were not just making a claim of common heritage with David, but they were giving to him a pledge of loyalty. In the same way, Adam's words were more than a claim of special commonality between himself and Eve. They also constituted a commitment to her—based on his will and not on the whims of his emotions.[2]

Man's Distortion of God's Plan

Unfortunately, the Fall greatly inhibited mankind's ability to live in a godly manner, even in our marriages. It particularly damaged our ability to stick to our commitments.

In the story of the Fall, you probably remember that the serpent came to Eve and asked her, "Indeed, has God said, 'You shall not eat from any tree of the garden'?" (Gen. 3:1). But did you know that Eve's response revealed a lack of commitment to God's instructions? Take a look at the command as God gave it to Adam:

---

2. Victor P. Hamilton, *The Book of Genesis Chapters 1–17,* The New International Commentary of the Old Testament series (Grand Rapids, Mich.: William B. Eerdmans Publishing Co., 1990), pp. 179–180.

"From any tree of the garden you may eat freely; but from the tree of the knowledge of good and evil you shall not eat, for in the day that you eat from it you will surely die." (2:16–17, emphasis added)

Now take a look at Eve's paraphrase of it:

"From the fruit of the trees of the garden we may eat; but from the fruit of the tree which is in the middle of the garden, God has said, 'You shall not eat from it or touch it, or you will die.'" (3:2–3)

It's almost the same thing, just with a slight—but significant—difference. God had said they could eat from *any* tree in the garden, except the one. Eve, though, described this freedom so matter-of-factly that it's hard to believe she appreciated it. "Ho-hum," she seems to say, "we only get to eat from the trees in the garden." What disdain for the incredible abundance God had laid before her and her man (see 1:29–30)!

Eve also seems to obsess on the one thing God had forbidden. The Lord had told her and Adam not to *eat* from the one tree. Eve, however, added that they were not to even *touch* it. Can't you just see her sitting on a grassy knoll, ignoring the beauty around her, staring addictively at the one thing she couldn't have? Ridiculous! Or it would be, if we hadn't done the same thing ourselves at times!

We all know the rest of the story—Eve and Adam ate the forbidden fruit and were evicted from the garden. But before God even found them out, right after they ate the fruit, an interesting thing happened:

Then the eyes of both of them were opened, and they knew that they were naked; and they sewed fig leaves together and made themselves loin coverings. (3:7)

From that moment forward, Adam and Eve's ability to honor their commitments became even more difficult. They no longer would need a serpent to lead them into iniquity; they now had sin natures, and those natures would continually whisper in their ears, "Eve's not looking as firm as she used to, but that girl down by the sheep gate—now she's a real looker!" or "Adam isn't as attentive toward me as he used to be. I wish he'd look at me the way Ahithaphel does when I go to buy fish from him at the market. Say, maybe I'll go and buy some fish today."

God's Plan for Restoration

Thankfully, God has provided us with a plan for restoration, a way to help us keep our commitments and allow us to experience the deepest depths of marital stability and intimacy.

God's Plan of Protection against Immorality

If there ever was an ancient culture that could match the immorality found in our modern Western societies, it was that of Corinth. "Corinthianizing" was a term used in the ancient world to describe the debaucheries practiced by vagrants, drunkards, and sexual deviants. The city was infamous as a center for moral laxity. Minus the neon, its streets were little different than the red light districts found today in every city and town of sizable population.

In his first letter to the Corinthian believers, Paul fought against this immorality, which, unfortunately, had seeped into the church. Among his instructions for fighting sinful practices, Paul offered marriage as a way for the Corinthian Christians to protect themselves from sexual promiscuity.

> Now concerning the things about which you wrote, it is good for a man not to touch a woman. But because of immoralities, each man is to have his own wife, and each woman is to have her own husband. (1 Cor. 7:1–2)

Paul's advice is extremely practical. In effect, he says, "Remember where you're living; remember that you reside in Corinth where you can't even walk down the street without temptation getting in your face. Remember that each one of you has a sex drive. It would be far better to marry than to commit adultery or fornication."

This sounds like a pretty low view of marriage, doesn't it? It sounds like Paul is prescribing marriage only as a preventative means against sexual sin. On the contrary, Paul had a very high view of marriage. In this case, however, he's merely facing reality. A man or woman not specifically called to a life of abstinence should not even attempt it. To do so would mean to place himself or herself deliberately in the path of unnecessary temptation.

In a very real and practical way, marriage is God's protection plan against immorality. That's something we need desperately in our Corinthian-like world today.

Additional "Insurance" for Married Couples

Marriage helps guard against immorality, but as we saw in the case of Adam and Eve, even the covenant of matrimony gives us no guarantee that we'll be able to maintain our commitments— not to God, and certainly not to each other. In order to help his married readers even more, Paul offers another lesson:

> The husband must fulfill his duty to his wife, and likewise also the wife to her husband. The wife does not have authority over her own body, but the husband does; and likewise also the husband does not have authority over his own body, but the wife does. Stop depriving one another, except by agreement for a time, so that you may devote yourselves to prayer, and come together again so that Satan will not tempt you because of your lack of self-control. (vv. 3–5)

Many Corinthians believed that the physical body was evil, that only the spirit was pure. As a result, many church members had decided to totally abstain from physical pleasures, especially sex. Paul, however, emphatically recommended that they continue to engage in healthy relations within the bounds of marriage.

Several details in Paul's advice are worth noting. First, he states that sexual intimacy is a "duty." Have you ever thought about sex in that way—as a duty you have to your spouse? By "duty," Paul meant "debt" or "what is owed."[3] The implication is that neither partner is free to withhold sex from the other. Sexual intimacy is a debt spouses owe to each other.

How can such a debt exist? Because, in marriage, we do not hold exclusive ownership over our bodies. Paul tells us that the husband has authority over his wife's body, and the wife has authority over her husband's. Each belongs to the other—they are their spouse's possession.

As a result, any period of sexual inactivity should be entered into deliberately and only by mutual consent. The husband and wife should agree to both the length and purpose of the sabbatical. What should that purpose be? Paul says, "so that you may devote yourselves to prayer." In other words, the reason should be spiritual, like

---

3. Curtis Vaughan and Thomas D. Lea, *1 Corinthians*, Bible Study Commentary series (Grand Rapids, Mich.: Lamplighter Books, 1983), p. 70.

praying for a child who has fallen into grievous sin, periods of soul-searching or seeking God's will, and times of repentance and renewal.

Finally, Paul commands the husband and wife to resume relations when the agreed-upon time has ended. Why? For the sake of sexual fidelity—so that they won't be tempted to gratify their sexual desires through sinful means.

One more thing. Let's remember that Paul was combating a specific problem in the Corinthian congregation—the aim of some people to totally abstain from sex. It was these people Paul was addressing, not those struggling with unhealthy or sinful attitudes in their marriages. For example, the apostle would never approve of his words being used by an abusive husband to demand sex from his wife, or any similar situation. People who are experiencing problems in their marriage should seek the help of a professional or pastoral counselor before they attempt to apply the truths of this lesson.

Disclaimers aside, do you see now how marriage—particularly sex in marriage—can act as "commitment insurance"? Consistent, healthy sexual intimacy helps keep us faithful to our mates and fulfill our commitment to them. And this long-lasting and deep sense of commitment to another human being helps us begin to understand and appreciate God's commitment to us. Yet it's only by experiencing God's character that we can hope to treat our spouses with that same love and loyalty. This is one of the mysteries of marriage.

🔗 Living Insights

Recently, an aged seminary professor, a widower, married a woman twenty-five years younger than himself. When asked about the possible impropriety of his act, he wryly replied, "I'd rather smell perfume than Ben-Gay any day."

Most of us probably haven't seen our spouses move into the "Ben-Gay" stage of life yet, but perhaps we've seen their bodies lose the shape of their youth. Maybe spare tires and love handles have replaced washboard abs and sculpted thighs. And maybe we're beginning to feel a little bit like the professor, longing for something better. Take the next few minutes to consider the state of sexual intimacy in your marriage—not what might be better, but what's *the best*.

How do you feel about sex in your marriage? Try to get rid of any unrealistic expectations you might have (for example, images from Hollywood films in which couples roll around passionately on a sandy beach—how uncomfortable!—or enjoy passionate sex despite severe emotional problems in their relationships).

Part of making a better marriage is becoming a better mate. What can you do to become a better lover? Ask your mate in what areas he or she would like to see improvement.

Have you allowed yourself to become so busy that you've failed to make regular payments on your "love debt" to your spouse? What can you do to improve your consistency?

Have you ever entered into an agreement with your spouse to abstain for awhile? If so, how did it go? What worked well? What will you do differently the next time you find the need to enter one of these periods?

Remember, God designed sex to be so good that it would act as glue to help keep marriages together. Sex alone can't save or preserve a sick relationship, but it can certainly help a healthy one stay that way.

Chapter 5

THE MYSTERY OF
LAWLESSNESS

2 Thessalonians 2:1–12

D o you ever fret about the future of this world, worry about how close we're getting to the wicked end? If you do, you've got plenty of fodder to fuel your cares and concerns.

These days, the earth is filled with evil, which many people take to be a sign that we're nearing the end times. And how can we argue with them? Look at the kind of people we've got walking around today. Dictators like Saddam Hussein carry out their agendas of conquest and oppression, not to mention terrorist groups that will do anything—anything—to get what they want. Brutal people, however, aren't the only problem.

Natural disasters seem more common than ticks on a blood-hound. Earthquakes, floods, forest fires, hurricanes, droughts, tornadoes —you name, we've got it. And there's more. . . .

Social upheaval has hit the headlines more than a few times in recent years—the slaughter of thousands in Rwanda, and the bloody conflicts between the Serbs, Croats, and Bosnians. And as usual, the Middle East continues to be a hotbed of turmoil.

With all this going on, who dares to say we're *not* nearing the end? As surprising as this may sound, turmoil is nothing new. Law-lessness, social and natural, has held the earth in its grip since the Fall. The people of this world have continually been afflicted by vicious despots (Nero and Vlad the Impaler, to name a couple), natural disasters (remember studying Pompeii and the Black Death?), and social strife (think of the Crusades and the fall of Rome).

Christians, in response, have always wondered if they were near-ing the dreaded Day of the Lord, in which God will pour out His wrath on mankind for our wickedness.[1] In fact, the very first be-lievers lived in fear of that day. Let's take a look at one example,

---

1. The "Day of the Lord" is a common expression in Scripture, used to describe the period of time in which God will deal with sin. This period of time will include the seven-year Tribulation, the second advent of Christ, and the millenial kingdom. The Day of the Lord will culminate in the Great White Throne Judgment.

the Thessalonian church, and read Paul's attempt to quell their fears. In his words, we'll discover what the apostle calls "the mystery of lawlessness," and we'll see how it can help us handle the storm of chaos that continually swirls around us today.

Fear in the First Century

The second chapter of 2 Thessalonians is one of the greatest prophetic passages in all of Scripture. No other chapter in the Bible covers precisely the same points of revelation that are given here. Paul wrote this letter because the Thessalonians believed they were living in the Day of the Lord, a judgment that Paul previously had told them they would miss.[2] And who can blame them for believing the end had come? They were practically being crushed by persecution from the Roman government.

The Day of the Lord Now?

The Thessalonians' fears arose from another letter they had received, supposedly from Paul himself, which stated that the Day of the Lord had arrived. Paul, however, quickly set the record straight.

> Now we request you, brethren, with regard to the coming of our Lord Jesus Christ and our gathering together to Him, that you not be quickly shaken from your composure or be disturbed either by a spirit or a message or *a letter as if from us*, to the effect that the day of the Lord has come. (2 Thess. 2:1–2, emphasis added)

Paul did not write any such letter, and he knew that the Day of the Lord had not yet arrived. Further, he didn't want the Thessalonians to become "shaken from their composure." This is an interesting phrase. As Ray Stedman notes:

> The phrase literally reads, "You were shaken out of your minds" or, to put it in the vernacular, "all shook up." Linked with this is a word that can only be translated "disturbed." (The same word is translated

2. In 1 Thessalonians 5:1–11, Paul tells them that the Day of the Lord would come like a thief in the night (v. 2), but that they would miss this event because they were not destined for wrath (v. 9).

"alarmed" in Mark 13:7 RSV.) They were not excited about the coming of the Lord. Rather, they were scared out of their minds! It was sweaty palms and white knuckles all the way![3]

Paul didn't want the Thessalonians to fear, but he would not have lied to them. If the Day of the Lord had actually come, they would have had plenty to be worried about. Thankfully, that time had not yet come. So Paul was able to comfort them. To further console them, the apostle offered proof that his words were true.

Events That Must Happen First

Before the Day of the Lord can come, two events must transpire. Paul continues:

> Let no one in any way deceive you, for it will not come unless the apostasy comes first, and the man of lawlessness is revealed, the son of destruction. (v. 3)

The first event that must precede the Day is called the apostasy. The Greek term, *apostasia*, is often rendered "falling away" or "rebellion." Leon Morris offers a detailed description of the word:

> The term rendered "rebellion" is sometimes used of political or military rebellions. The characteristic thought of the Bible is that God rules. Thus the word is appropriate for a rebellion against his rule. In part "rebellion" points to this sort of thing; it includes the idea of forsaking one's former allegiance. But it is not so much forsaking one's first love and drifting into apathy that is meant, as setting oneself actively in opposition to God. . . . Paul does not speak of "a" rebellion, as though introducing the topic for the first time, but of "the" rebellion, that is, the well-known rebellion, that one about which he had already instructed them.[4]

---

3. Ray C. Stedman, *Waiting for the Second Coming: Studies in Thessalonians* (Grand Rapids, Mich.: Discovery House Publishers, 1990), p. 123.

4. Leon Morris, *The First and Second Epistles to the Thessalonians*, rev. ed., ed. F. F. Bruce, The New International Commentary on the New Testament series (Grand Rapids, Mich.: William B. Eerdmans Publishing Co., 1991), pp. 218–219.

So the Day of the Lord will not come until this mass rebellion takes place. Although the last few years of the twentieth century have seen an increase in opposition to God, we still have yet to witness the kind of falling away described by Paul.

In addition to the apostasy, the "man of lawlessness" must also be revealed. In fact, this man will lead the rebellion against God. He'll be called the "man of lawlessness" because anarchy will characterize his life and impact on the world. And look what he'll do:

> [He] opposes and exalts himself above every so-called god or object of worship, so that he takes his seat in the temple of God, displaying himself as being God. (v. 4)

This act refers to the "abomination of desolation," in which the Antichrist, during the Tribulation, will sit on the throne in the rebuilt temple of Jerusalem, setting himself up as God. Jesus Himself prophesied that this would happen (see Matt. 24:15–28).[5]

Since the temple of Jerusalem had not yet been rebuilt—and remains unbuilt to this day—the Thessalonians could rest assured as we can, that the Day of the Lord is yet to come.

Provision in the Present

The Day of the Lord has not yet arrived because the "Restrainer" remains on the earth, who holds back the tide of unbridled evil that the man of lawlessness will bring.

> And you know what restrains him [man of lawlessness] now, so that in his time he will be revealed. For the mystery of lawlessness is already at work; only he who now restrains will do so until he is taken out of the way. (vv. 6–7)

Who is this Restrainer? Scholars have a hard time agreeing. Even conservative expositors who interpret the Scriptures literally disagree. The most likely interpretation for the Restrainer is either:

---

5. The term "Antichrist" is used only once in the Bible (1 John 2:13), but the man described by this name is called other things as well, particularly "man of lawlessness" (2 Thess. 2:3), "the beast" (Rev. 13; 17), and "little horn" (Dan. 7:8). Although neither Jesus nor Paul mention the Antichrist explicitly, he is clearly the one they had in mind. For further discussion, see Paul N. Benware, *Understanding End Times Prophecy* (Chicago, Ill.: Moody Press, 1995), pp. 249–50.

one, the presence of governments that generally uphold the law (see Rom. 13:1–7 and 1 Pet. 2:13–17) or two, the Holy Spirit who indwells all believers living on the earth.

The most likely option appears to be the Holy Spirit. After all, He is the One who ultimately restrains evil, which He does through us who are called to be the salt—preservative—of this earth (Matt. 5:13). Paul tells us that the man of lawlessness cannot come until the Restrainer is taken out of the way. In other words, the Antichrist can't appear until the church is raptured.

Until that time, we live under the "mystery of lawlessness." Morris renders the phrase this way:

> "The secret power of lawlessness" is an unusual expression. The word translated "secret power" (and more usually "mystery") in the New Testament has nothing of the mysteriousness in our sense of the term about it (nor, for that matter, of power). It denotes rather that which is secret, which is hidden from people, and which people, for all their searching, will never find by their own efforts. Usually there is the added thought that the mystery has now been made known. It is not surprising that it is normally employed of the purposes of God in salvation and the like. The mystery involved in the gospel was not known and could not be known until God pleased to reveal it in Christ (e.g., Rom. 16:25–26). But the use of the term here reminds us that there are secrets as well in sin. We can never, by our own reasoning, plumb the depths of iniquity, the reason for its existence, or the manner of its working. Paul points out that even as he writes there is a secret activity of lawlessness at work. The explanation of it all is not open to us, but the fact of its being in operation is clear enough. The use of the term "lawlessness" connects it with the Man of Lawlessness. Though that individual has not yet been revealed, the principle that governs his operations is already at work on this earth (cf. 1 John 2:18). It is probable that Paul does not mean simply that evil is at work. That has always been true. It is rather "the spirit of the antichrist" (1 John 4:3) that is in mind, a special

form of evil that is hostile to all that Christ stands for. We can scarcely be more specific in view of the reserve with which Paul writes. The verb rendered "is . . . at work" usually denotes some supernatural force. . . . Here it is Satan who sets "the mystery of lawlessness" in motion.[6]

Although we live in a time when "the spirit of the antichrist" works and moves among us, we have the provision of the Holy Spirit who, through us, restrains evil. This arrangement, however, will not always be the case.

The Coming Lawlessness

After the Restrainer is removed, the man of lawlessness will step into the limelight and take over. Paul goes into greater detail about this man and those who will follow him.

Then that lawless one will be revealed whom the Lord will slay with the breath of His mouth and bring to an end by the appearance of His coming; that is, the one who is coming is in accord with the activity of Satan, with all power and signs and false wonders, and with all the deception of wickedness for those who perish, because they did not receive the love of the truth so as to be saved. For this reason God will send upon them a deluding influence so that they will believe what is false, in order that they may be judged who did not believe the truth, but took pleasure in wickedness. (vv. 8–12)

In these words, Paul tells us that the lawless one's (the man of lawlessness) power will come from Satan himself, and Satan will enable him to perform many signs and deceptive wonders. As a result, he'll receive the world's admiration and they'll proclaim of him, "Who is like the beast?" (Rev. 13:4).

Those who follow him will be unbelievers, having rejected "the love of the truth so as to be saved." God will allow these people to fall under the lawless one's deluding influence in such a way that

---

6. Morris, *The First and Second Epistles to the Thessalonians*, pp. 228–229.

they'll believe whatever lies he tells them.[7] He'll lead them into wickedness, and they'll love it.

In the end, though, the man of lawlessness will be slain and his followers will be judged. Before all this happens—in the meantime —how would God like us to conduct ourselves?

Questions for Living in the Present

We need to ask ourselves four questions, which will help us make sure we're living as we should during this time characterized by the mystery of lawlessness.

First, *are you confident or confused about God's plan for the future?* If you don't know God's road map for the future, you're bound to wander aimlessly the way the Thessalonians did. Knowing the course of coming events will save you from the fears that often accompany ignorance.

Second, *are you ready for the rapture?* Christ can take us at any moment. Have you believed in Christ for the forgiveness of your sin? Are you living by faith, expecting His arrival?

Third, *are you helping the Holy Spirit restrain the evil around you?* Refuse to gossip when those around you start talking behind someone's back. Refrain from constant complaining, even when things are going badly. Don't criticize unless it will be truly constructive. Little things like these can help the Spirit restrain evil.

Fourth, *are you discerning or gullible when the subject of the supernatural comes up?* People will follow the Antichrist because of the supernatural signs he will perform. And these people will probably think that *they* are the *true* believers, since their leader will proclaim to be the Christ and will sit on the throne in the temple. We, on the other hand, should use discernment. Not every miracle performed in Christ's name comes from Him (see Matt. 7:15–23).

Do you fear that we're nearing the Day of the Lord? We may or may not be, but there's nothing to fear. We have the Holy Spirit, and when He leaves, we'll leave also. We'll be raptured into the sky and united with Christ. Only then will the man of lawlessness come. Until that day, we can live as restrainers, fighting evil during the mystery of lawlessness.

---

7. God Himself will not deceive them, but He will give them over to their own sin and allow them to believe what they want to hear.

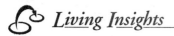 *Living Insights*

Continuing our discussion of how to be restrainers, let's look at Christ's description of how believers can act as salt and light in society:

> "You are the salt of the earth; but if the salt has become tasteless, how can it be made salty again? It is no longer good for anything, except to be thrown out and trampled under foot by men."
>
> "You are the light of the world. A city set on a hill cannot be hidden; nor does anyone light a lamp and put it under a basket, but on the lampstand, and it gives light to all who are in the house. Let your light shine before men in such a way that they may see your good works, and glorify your Father who is in heaven." (Matt. 5:13–16)

Did you notice *how* our light is supposed to shine, *how* our salt is supposed to flavor and preserve? We should do our good works in such a way that others notice them, and as a result, glorify God— have a high view of Him. In other words, we're supposed to be good witnesses.

Name the unbeliever in your life with whom you have the most contact: _____

What can you do or say that will make you better salt or a brighter light to him or her?

_____

_____

_____

_____

_____

_____

_____

_____

_____

_____

Chapter 6

THE MYSTERY OF
CHRIST'S RETURN

1 Corinthians 15:50–57; 1 Thessalonians 4:13–18; Titus 2:11–13

In this study guide, we've discussed the aspects of our faith that the Bible calls mysteries. So far, we've examined the mysteries of God Himself, the gospel, marriage, and the lawlessness to come. Now let's discuss the final mystery—the one surrounding Christ's return.

Like the other mysteries, Christ's return is not a mystery in the sense that it is hard to understand. Rather, it's a reality hidden to the uninitiated—a secret revealed only to Christ's followers. Here's what Christ Himself revealed about His future coming:

> "Do not let your heart be troubled; believe in God, believe also in Me. In My Father's house are many dwelling places; if it were not so, I would have told you; for I go to prepare a place for you. If I go and prepare a place for you, I will come again and receive you to Myself, that where I am, there you may be also." (John 14:1–3)

How comforting to know that Christ will come back for us! At least, it *should* be comforting. Is it for you? Or do you, like the Corinthian and Thessalonian believers, have some questions and concerns that trouble you? Do you wonder, as they did, what has happened to those who have already died? Or about unbelievers? Or about those who will be alive when He returns? The unknowns surrounding the mystery of Christ's coming actually caused the Thessalonians to fear this event, just as it does many believers today.

Before we see how Paul quieted the Thessalonians' concerns, let's first clarify two concepts relating to all of them.

Two Clarifications concerning Death and Destiny

What happens when we die? Where do our souls go at the

This chapter has been adapted from "Watching for Jesus in the Air" in the study guide *The Majesty of God's Son*, coauthored by Jason Shepherd, from the Bible-teaching ministry of Charles R. Swindoll (Anaheim, Calif.: Insight for Living, 1999).

moment of our deaths? Two concepts lie beneath these questions—death and destiny.

Death

Death is not an ending. Rather, it's a separation. The soul—that invisible part of us that gives us life and personality—separates from our body. The body ceases to function, or dies, but the soul lives on forever.

Destiny

Where does the soul go once death has evicted it from its home? Scripture teaches us that the souls of believers go to live in the presence of the Lord (2 Cor. 5:8; Luke 16:22; 23:43). The souls of unbelievers, however, go to *hades*, also called hell—a place of suffering (16:22–23). Nowhere does Scripture teach the concept of purgatory. Rather, it teaches that a person's destiny is sealed upon death. We will not have the opportunity to change our destinies once we've died.

Perishable Transformed into Imperishable

So, if Christ is coming back for all who believe in Him, both those still living and those who have died, what is He going to do about our perishable bodies, if anything? In 1 Corinthians 15:50–57, Paul reveals the answer.

Answering an Underlying Question

Paul has already explained in 1 Corinthians 15:35–49 that the dead in Christ will be raised, and he has described the nature of their resurrection bodies. But what about those who are still alive on that resurrection day? Will they remain in their earthly bodies? This must have weighed heavily on the Corinthian believers' minds. So Paul explains to them, beginning in verse 50.

> Now I say this, brethren, that flesh and blood cannot inherit the kingdom of God; nor does the perishable inherit the imperishable.

Simply stated, nothing perishable is equipped to endure eternity. Therefore, even those who are alive when Christ comes will receive new bodies. This is the mystery Paul wants us to understand:

> Behold, I tell you a mystery; we will not all sleep [die], but we will all be changed. (v. 51)

45

Those who have died will be resurrected to receive their new bodies, and those still living will get their new bodies as well. Is this a long, gradual process? Not at all, as Paul explains next.

The Suddenness of Our Transformation

Our transformation from perishable to imperishable will occur suddenly. Paul says it will happen "in a moment, in the twinkling of an eye" (v. 52a). The Greek term for "moment," *atomos*, means "uncut" or "indivisible because of smallness"; and the phrase for "in the twinkling of an eye," *en ripe opthalmou*, conveys the same idea as the English phrase "in the blink of an eye."[1]

How It Will Occur

What will signal this sudden event? Paul describes that next:

> For the trumpet will sound, and the dead will be raised imperishable, and we will be changed. (v. 52b)

In 1 Thessalonians, which we'll examine more closely later in this chapter, Paul adds that an angel will shout prior to the trumpet blast. So, the order of events for the Rapture will be as follows:

- An angel will shout,

- a trumpet will be heard,

- the dead believers will be raised first,

- and then the living will be changed.

Whether living or dead, however, *all* will be transformed.

The Need to Be Transformed

Paul reiterates the necessity of transformation prior to entering God's presence:

> For this perishable must put on the imperishable, and this mortal must put on immortality. (v. 53)

Perishable flesh simply cannot mix with God's immortal kingdom; so we not only *will* be changed—we *must* be changed. Then something grand will occur.

1 Gordon D. Fee, *The First Epistle to the Corinthians*, The New International Commentary on the New Testament series (Grand Rapids, Mich.: William B. Eerdmans Publishing Co., 1987), p. 801.

Victory over Death!

Our transformation at the Rapture not only gives us immortal life, but it also defeats death.

> But when this perishable will have put on the imperishable, and this mortal will have put on immortality, then will come about the saying that is written, "Death is swallowed up in victory. O death, where is your victory? O death, where is your sting?" The sting of death is sin, and the power of sin is the law; but thanks be to God, who gives us the victory through our Lord Jesus Christ. (vv. 54–57)

When we are made new in Christ, our age-old enemy, death, will be the conquered, not the conqueror. Death will stalk us no more, cause no more pain and sorrow. Commentators Curtis Vaughan and Thomas D. Lea tell us that "in speaking of the 'sting' of death, the apostle depicts death as a venomous serpent inflicting fatal wounds. Christ, however, has drawn its sting and left it powerless."[2] Thanks be to God, indeed, for graciously allowing us to share in Christ's victory over death!

Be Informed . . . Be Comforted

As a result of Paul's teachings on the Rapture, some first-century believers reacted in extremes. The Thessalonian church was particularly plagued by this problem. Ecstatic about Christ's imminent return and their future transformation, some Thessalonian believers quit their jobs and awaited the Rapture in idleness. Also troubling the church was a lot of misinformation. The people were afraid their departed loved ones would be forgotten by Christ when He returned. So Paul, in his first letter to them, gave them a detailed explanation.

Regarding Our Death and Life Afterward

Affirming the need for Christians to understand these truths, Paul begins:

> We do not want you to be uninformed, brethren, about those who are asleep. (1 Thess. 4:13a)

2. Curtis Vaughan and Thomas D. Lea, *1 Corinthians*, Bible Study Commentary series (Grand Rapids, Mich.: Zondervan Publishing House, Lamplighter Books, 1983), p. 164.

Asleep describes death. It is a hopeful word, because sleeping assumes a temporary rest and a future awakening—a resurrection. Motivating Paul's words is his pastoral concern "that you will not grieve as do the rest who have no hope" (v. 13b).

Paul says we don't have to grieve without hope. Notice, however, that he doesn't say we're not supposed to grieve at all. Don't let people tell you that strong Christians don't weep when death claims a loved one. The fact is, not until we experience the emotional depths of grief can we step into life's fullness again. We must "walk *through* the valley of the shadow of death" before we can reach the other side (Ps. 23:4a, emphasis added). But through that valley, God is beside us, reminding us of the eternal sunshine beyond the grieving and the grave.

The basis of our hope is that "Jesus died and rose again" (1 Thess. 4:14a)—the most significant statement in Scripture. Through His atoning sacrifice and His grave-defeating resurrection, Christ has conquered sin and death. As a result,

> if we believe that Jesus died and rose again, even so God will bring with Him those who have fallen asleep in Jesus. (v. 14)

There's that word again, *asleep*. As Paul unfolds the subject of the resurrection and Rapture, he makes it clear that God will arouse the sleeping bodies of dead believers.

Regarding Christ's Coming and Others' Joining

Paul next sets out the order of events surrounding the resurrection, this time including the Rapture too.

> For this we say to you by the word of the Lord, that we who are alive and remain until the coming of the Lord, will not precede those who have fallen asleep. For the Lord Himself will descend from heaven with a shout, with the voice of the archangel and with the trumpet of God, and the dead in Christ will rise first. Then we who are alive and remain will be caught up together with them in the clouds to meet the Lord in the air, and so we shall always be with the Lord. (vv. 15–17)

We, like the Thessalonians, have nothing to fear concerning our loved ones who have died in Christ. They will be the first

Christ gathers to Himself. Then those who are alive will follow. What a family reunion that will be! Husbands and wives, parents and children, friends and relatives separated by death will join hands once again to live forever, together with Christ. All of this will happen *before* the Day of the Lord comes. So we have nothing to fear about the future.

Regarding Confidence and Comfort

"Therefore," Paul concludes, "comfort one another with these words" (v. 18). His words are for the fearful, who wonder if Christ has forgotten the dead; for the unsure, who wonder what lies beyond the grave; and for the grieving, who think the last rose on the coffin must be the final good-bye. Christ has not forgotten; eternal life is free; and death is only sleep.

Responding to Christ's Coming

In light of what we've learned, we must ask ourselves, "What does it mean to prepare for Christ's coming? How do I respond to this?" Paul provides direction in a letter to his friend Titus:

> For the grace of God has appeared, bringing salvation to all men, instructing us to deny ungodliness and worldly desires and to live sensibly, righteously and godly in the present age, looking for the blessed hope and the appearing of the glory of our great God and Savior, Christ Jesus. (Titus 2:11–13)

From this passage, we can draw four practical responses. First, *make certain you have taken what God has given—His salvation*. Christ died to pay for your sins and rose to give you eternal life. To be forgiven and to receive life, He asks simply that you place your belief in Him. Have you?

Second, *continue to resist a corrupt lifestyle*. Paul instructs us to "deny ungodliness and worldly desires" so we won't be caught unprepared. Are you?

Third, *live in a sensible, godly manner*. Live as if Christ might come today. Stay involved in Christ's program; give yourself to the Savior; share His love with others. Do you?

Fourth, *from now on, keep watching for Jesus in the air*. Like a child on Christmas Eve, anticipate His coming and the gifts He will bring. Remind yourself of the blessed hope to come. Will you?

 *Living Insights*

What can we do now that we understand the mystery of Christ's return? Let's look through the following Scriptures to discover some ways to keep focusing heavenward.

According to the following verses, what benefits await Christians at Christ's coming?

2 Corinthians 5:1–5 _____

_____

_____

1 Peter 1:3–5 _____

_____

_____

What should be our attitudes toward Christ's coming?

Philippians 3:20 _____

_____

_____

2 Timothy 4:8 _____

_____

_____

What actions characterize those who are keeping ready?

Romans 13:11–14 _____

_____

_____

Philippians 4:5 _____

_____

_____

James 5:8–9 _____

_____

_____

1 Peter 4:7–11 _____

_____

_____

Suppose Christ told you He was planning to come at midnight to-morrow. How would that knowledge affect your relationship with God?

_____

_____

How would it affect the way you relate to others? _____

_____

_____

How would it affect the way you feel about yourself? _____

_____

_____

Christ could come tomorrow at midnight. He may even come before you finish reading this sentence. What changes should you make to better prepare for the Rapture?

_____

_____

_____

BOOKS FOR PROBING FURTHER

How can we possibly plumb the depths of God's mysteries in six short studies? It's impossible! These mysteries are too vast, too deep, too profound to be fully examined in one guide or book. So, to help you dig even deeper, we'd like to suggest the following books.

God

Boa, Kenneth. *Unraveling the Big Questions about God*. Grand Rapids, Mich.: Zondervan Publishing House, Lamplighter Books, 1988.

Swindoll, Charles R. *The Mystery of God's Will*. Nashville, Tenn.: Word Publishing, 1999.

Tozer, A. W. *The Knowledge of the Holy*. San Francisco, Calif.: Harper and Row, Publishers, 1961.

The Gospel and Christian Life

Colson, Charles with Ellen Santilli Vaughn. *The Body*. Dallas, Tex.: Word Publishing, 1992.

Peterson, Eugene. *A Long Obedience in the Same Direction*. Downers Grove, Ill.: InterVarsity Press, 1980.

Zacharias, Ravi. *Deliver Us from Evil*. Dallas, Tex.: Word Publishing, 1996.

Marriage

Crabb, Larry. *The Marriage Builder*. Grand Rapids, Mich.: Zondervan Publishing House, 1992.

Smalley, Gary with John Trent. *Love Is a Decision*. Dallas, Tex.: Word Publishing, 1989.

Willard F. Harley Jr., *His Needs, Her Needs*. Grand Rapids, Mich.: Baker Book House, Fleming H. Revell Co., 1988.

End Times

Benware, Paul N. *Understanding End Times Prophecy*. Chicago, Ill.: Moody Press, 1995.

Dyer, Charles H. with Angela Elwell Hunt *The Rise of Babylon*. Wheaton, Ill.: Tyndale House Publishers, 1991.

Walvoord, John F. *The Prophecy Knowledge Handbook*. Wheaton, Ill.: Scripture Press Publications, Victor Books, 1990.

Some of these books may be out of print and available only through a library. For those currently available, please contact your local Christian bookstore. Books by Charles R. Swindoll, as well as some books by other authors, may be obtained through Insight for Living.

Insight for Living offers study guides on many books of the Bible, as well as on a variety of issues and biblical personalities. For more information, see the ordering instructions at the back of this guide and contact the office that serves you.

NOTES

NOTES

NOTES

NOTES

ORDERING INFORMATION

DISCOVERING GOD'S MYSTERIES

If you would like to order additional study guides, purchase the cassette series that accompanies this guide, or request our product catalogs, please contact the office that serves you.

United States and International locations:

Insight for Living
Post Office Box 69000
Anaheim, CA 92817-0900

1-800-772-8888, 24 hours a day, seven days a week
(714) 575-5000, 8:00 A.M. to 4:30 P.M., Pacific time, Monday to Friday

Canada:

Insight for Living Ministries
Post Office Box 2510
Vancouver, BC, Canada V6B 3W7

1-800-663-7639, 24 hours a day, seven days a week

Australia:

Insight for Living, Inc.
General Post Office Box 2823 EE
Melbourne, VIC 3001, Australia

Toll-free 1800-772-888 or (03) 9877-4277, 8:30 A.M. to 5:00 P.M., Monday to Friday

World Wide Web:

www.insight.org

Study Guide Subscription Program

Study guide subscriptions are available. Please call or write the office nearest you to find out how you can receive our study guides on a regular basis.